Table of Contents

I've done that,

wanted that,

been that,

battled that,

cried over that,

had that,

loved that,

and

lost that...

all the reasons

I drink to that!

MASTERING CONCOCTOLOGY   0-1

Tools and Equipment
Turn a serving for one into a pitcher
How to Rim a Cocktail Glass
How to Chill a Cocktail Glass
How to Mix a Martini
Chocolate Shavings

INFUSED SPIRITS   2-3

Green Apple Infused Vodka
Basil Infused Vodka
Candy Corn Infused Vodka
Apple Jolly Rancher Infused Vodka
Strawberry Starburst Infusion
Pineapple Infused Vodka
Peppercorn Infused Vodka
Jalapeno Chili Infusion
Serrano Chili Infusion
Habanero Chili Infusion
Berry Good Infused Vodka
Bloody Mary Vodka Infusion

INFUSION = COLLUSION   4-5

Berry Good Lemonade
Starburst-tini
Project Pineapple 101
Pucker Up and Kiss Me-tini
Mama Caliente
Basil Lemon Drop
Rock My Boat Girlie-tini
Apple Jolly Rancher
Caliente Girlie-tini

LIQUORS AND MIXERS 6-7

Limoncello
Moonshine
Coffee Liqueur
Amaretto
Irish Cream
Cranberry Mixer
Simple Syrup
Sweet and Sour Mix

BLOODY MARY AND HER ENTOURAGE 8-9

Bloody Rich Mary
Twisted Bloody Mary Mix
Moody Mary
Blonde Mary
Sinful Mary
Harry Carry Mary

CHAMPAGNE GIGGLES 10-11

Pink Princess
The Dazzler
Lemony Fizz
Razzamatazz
Bellissimo
Paradise Fizz
Mmmmmmmmimosa
Southern Bella Bellini
Peaches and Crème Bellini
Pink Fizzy
Cranberry Fizz

MARDI GRAS 12-13

Heracame
Himacame
Masked Lady
Blue Bayou
French Quarter Fizz
Cajun Martini
Carpe Diem
Mardi Gras Kiss

BESTIES 14-15

Bestie
Ya Yas
Caro Amico
Soul Sister-tini
Sassy Frassy
Mon Ami
Partners in Crime
Clique-tini
Birthday Girlie-tini

YAPPY HOUR 16-17

Pomegranate Girlie-tini
Liquid Courage
Hypno-Yolo
Key Lime Time-tini
Celebration-tini
Plan B
In Kahoots Girlie-tini
Peared-Up Girlie-tini

GROUP THERAPY — 18-19

Hell Ya
My Therapist
Tinky Tinglers
Group Therapy
Attitude Adjustment
Covert Mission
Operation Recovery
Happy Juice

IT'S BEEN A HELLAVA DAY — 20-21

50 Shades of Blue
Hellava Day
Middle Finger
#phecalphreak
PMS
It's a Loong Story
Bamboozled
WTF
50 Shades of Red

ATTITUDE ADJUSTMENT — 22-23

Time Out
Naughty Girl
Decompression
Mommy Water
Hell Ya
#berrysmashed
#begenerous
It's All About Me

TAKING MY BEST SHOT — 24-25

Yowza
Party Girl Shooter
Transformation
Woman's Honor
Slutty Professor
Red Headed Floozie
Birthday Cake
Kapowwww
Hot Damn!

THE YOUNG & THE RECKLESS — 26-27

#karaaaazygirlietini
#girlshavingfun
#selfietini
#ms.snarky
#partygirls
#winkydinkytini
#craycraygirlietini
#twofacedgirlietini
#twittermetini
#twistedtini

THE BREAK UP — 28-29

Psycho
Oxymoron
Dirty Bastard
Mr. Evil
Jekyll and Hyde
Wrecking Ball
Douche Bag
Painkiller

SUMMERTIME HEATWAVE   30-31

Easy Peasy Lemon Squeezy
Key Lime Dream
Buzz Patrol
Spiked Granita
Slushy Hussy
Risky Whiskey Slush
Delizioso
Summer Cooler
Sun-Kissed All Over
Jiggle Juice

GIRLIE-RITAS SENORITAS   32-33

Sinfull-rita
Twisted-rita
Fiesty-rita
Flirty Girlie-rita
Strawberry Girlie-rita
Sorbet-rita
Covert Mission Girlie-rita
Guava Jalapeno Girlie-rita
Girlie-rita Sweet and Sour Mix

SASSY GIRLS SANGRIAS   34-35

Oh So Easy Sangria
Berry-licious Sangria
Silly Girl Sangria
Sassy Sangria
Party Hardy Sangria
Beach Baby Sangria
Ma-Ma-Mia-Sangria
Sangria Sangria Sangria
Just Peachy Sangria

FEELING PUNCHY   36-37

Any Time Punch
Bunko Brew
Girls Gone Wild
Lil' Bit of Fun
Rumalicious Punch
Risky Whiskey Sour Punch
Themacame Punch

DESSERT ME   38-39

Guilty Pleasure
Strawberry Shortcake
Lemon Pie-Girlie-tini
Dessertedly Yummy
Muddy Buddy
Sin-Upon
Dirty Fool
Naughty Bedtime Story
OMG
Nite Cap

MY CHOCOLATE AFFAIR   40-41

Operation Damsel in Distress
Cardinal Sin
Ca-raazy Corruption
Almond Toffee Martini
Toffee Syrup
Whiskey Business
Mounds of Joy Girlie-tini
Feeling Kooky

COFFEE WITH NECESSARY VARIABLES   42-43

Royal Frappe
Sweet Insanity
Dominatrix
Necessary Variables
Nutty Girl Coffee
Chocolate Eclair

There are two types of people in this world; people you want to drink with and people who make you want to drink.

*Given a cape, cocktail and tiara, we
are sure we could save the world.*

*We are in between the stages of "The Young and Reckless"
and the "Old and Senseless" and we are
enjoying every minute of it!*

Why We Need Cocktails

Many call it "Happy Hour". We call it "Group Therapy". These weekly sessions are what keep us sane. I mean, after a stressful day at work or with toddlers, teenagers and a hubby, who doesn't need an "Attitude Adjustment"? There's usually 6-10 of us, ages 27-65, and it's our opportunity to get advice, give advice, share secrets, and to celebrate our good news or commiserate over our not so good news. Sometimes we meet at our favorite drinking establishment, but most of the time we host therapy sessions at one of our homes. As part of our therapy Eileen and I began concocting cocktails for the group and would name them to match whatever the hot topic was during the evening. When one of our besties was going through a breakup we mixed a bourbon concoction and called it SOB after the schmuck that was causing her heartache. If someone had experienced a Hellava Day, that was our inspiration for the cocktails, Middle Finger, and WTF. Therapy couldn't get any better than this. So there you have it, our inspiration for "Concoctology 101".

Let's face it, there are a million reasons to have a cocktail besides group therapy. There are celebrations, holiday gatherings, happy hour, dinner out, dinner in, girls night out, girls night in, you're by the pool, you have a husband and kids and your kids have kids, there's that wicked boss, you've had a "Hellava Day," or it was a heavenly day...so you need to celebrate or just unwind. Perhaps Mr. Right just broke your heart or Mr. Wrong just proposed. As you can see the list goes on and on. Cocktail hour is a social phenomenon where we connect with others, loosen up, and perhaps leave behind that burdensome baggage we carry day to day. There's just something about sharing a cocktail with others that can put us in a "Zen" state where for a certain amount of time everything is about relaxing, sharing, and having some fun.

We've concocted these cocktails you can share with your BFFs to toast to those occasions that are the good, the bad and the ugly because with our besties we can bare our hearts and souls, be snarky, honest, and even occasionally get sound advice. We've spent countless hours concocting cocktails that we hope will sooth your soul, make you giggle with delight, or will help to take the edge off some annoying kink in your life. Our philosophy is, "If you think it, drink it!" We hope you have as much fun concocting these drinks with your friends as we have.

Clink, drink and enjoy! And don't forget....drink responsibly!

Kim Car-bo-naughty & Eileen Be-on-key

Mastering Concoctology

Con-coct-o-lo-gy   n. The study of concocting cocktails for pleasure.

101

TOOLS AND EQUIPMENT

Bar Spoon: This long handled spoon is perfect for stirring and its spiraled handle can be used as a crushing device for ingredients needed to flavor drinks. Turning the spoon over allows the gentle pouring required to layer drinks. The end of the spoon can also be used for muddling herbs.

Blender, Magic Bullet or Food Processor: Necessary for blending drinks or crushing ice.

Channel Knife: A special tool used for creating citrus strips.

Cocktail Shaker: This is the most necessary piece of equipment for any concoctologist. We recommend you choose a shaker with the built-in strainer and a tightly fitted top. A shaker's purpose is to chill the drink while you blend a mixture of ingredients.

Juice Squeezer: A tool used to extract juice from fruit.

Muddler: This is used to crush or muddle fruits, herbs, sugars or other ingredients which releases fruits' juices and oils for maximum flavor.

Shot Glass or Jigger: When preparing a drink, use a shot glass with measurements or a jigger. Guessing can cause over pouring and could possibly ruin your drink.

Other essential items: bottle opener, can opener, cutting board, measuring cups and spoons, paring knife, mixing pitcher, vegetable peeler, zester, ice bucket, tongs, strainer and towels.

HOW TO TURN A SERVING FOR ONE INTO A PITCHER

Substitute ounce for cup, so if a drink recipe says 1 ounce, use 1 cup. If it says ½ ounce, use ½ cup.

HOW TO RIM A COCKTAIL GLASS

Margarita or Citrus Cocktail

Moisten the rim of your glass using a lemon or lime wedge.

Use a shallow plate or container large enough to fit the rim of the glass and pour margarita or a coarse sea salt into the dish. Dip your moistened glass rim into the salt and make sure it is thoroughly covered.

Martini or cocktail glasses

Use any of these to moisten the rim of your glass: simple syrup, honey, corn syrup, agave syrup, fruit juices, chocolate or caramel syrups. Usually anything sticky will work.

Pour the liquid into a shallow plate large enough to fit the rim of your glass. Dip your glass into the liquid and make sure it is thoroughly covered.

In a second shallow plate, pour any of the following to use for glass rimming: colored sugars, shredded coconut, cupcake sprinkles or jimmies, crushed candies or cookies, Pop Rocks, or Kool-aid. Dip your moistened glass into your rimming sugar.

HOW TO CHILL A COCKTAIL GLASS

Moisten your glass rim then add your rimming sugar. Set your glass in the refrigerator until your drink is ready to be served. This works exceptionally well when using chocolate syrup for rimming or for creating a decorative design inside the glass.

You can also fill your glass with ice while you mix your drink. Discard the ice then strain your drink into the glass.

Here's a toast to the friends and family I love...and these Girlie-Tinis that make this possible.

HOW TO MIX A MARTINI

cocktail ingredients
cocktail shaker
preferably crushed ice (or cubes)
jigge or shot glass
measuring spoons

First, prepare your Martini glass by rimming the edge of the glass. You can also add ice to your glass to chill it. Then discard the ice right before straining the drink into the glass.

Fill the shaker half way with crushed ice. Add measured ingredients to your cocktail shaker. Make sure the cap is secure, then hold the cap and shaker while you shake the crap out of it until the drink is well blended and chilled. You want a frost to form on the outside of the shaker.

Remove the cap and strain the drink into your prepared glass. The perfect martini will have a float of ice on top. Add your garnish.

CHOCOLATE SHAVINGS

Create the chocolate shavings using a frozen dark chocolate bar and a vegetable peeler. Shave the chocolate off the bar the same way you would remove the skin from a carrot.

1

INFUSed spirits

GREEN APPLE INFUSED VODKA

2 cups vodka

1 Granny Smith green apple

Peel and slice the apple, excluding core, and add to a wide mouth mason jar. Cover with vodka, seal and infuse in the refrigerator for 48 hours. Strain out apple and continue storing in the refrigerator until ready to use.

BASIL INFUSED VODKA

2 cups vodka

1 cup fresh basil leaves

Clean basil leaves and air dry. Infuse basil and vodka for a 24 hour period or longer in a sealed jar or container. Strain out basil leaves and continue storing vodka in a cool place until ready to use.

CANDY CORN INFUSED VODKA

2 cups vodka

one-half bag candy corn

Infuse vodka and candy corn until candy is dissolved. Strain out candy residue. Store until ready to use.

APPLE JOLLY RANCHER INFUSED VODKA

2 cups vodka

12 unwrapped Apple Jolly Ranchers

Infuse until the candy is dissolved. Store in a sealed container until ready to use. Try different flavors.

STRAWBERRY STARBURST INFUSION

1 cup vodka

6 unwrapped strawberry Starburst

Infuse until the Starburst are dissolved. (24 hours) Strain out sediment. Pour infused vodka into a sealed jar and store in a cool place until ready to use. Try different flavors.

PINEAPPLE INFUSED VODKA

1 bottle (750 ml) vodka

1 fresh pineapple, cubed

Put cubed pineapple into a large container, then cover with vodka. Seal and infuse in the refrigerator for 72 hours. Refrigerate until ready to use.

JOLLY RANCHER BLUE RASPBERRY, CHERRY, AND APPLE INFUSED VODKAS

PEPPERCORN INFUSED VODKA

2 cups vodka
2 teaspoons peppercorns

Combine 2 teaspoons of peppercorns and vodka in a jar, seal, and infuse for 48 hours. Remove peppercorns and store in a cool place until ready to use. (Using white peppercorns will keep the vodka from turning black.)

JALAPENO CHILI INFUSION

3 cups vodka, rum, gin, or tequila
1 jalapeno pepper

Clean and slice 1 jalapeno. Infuse alcohol and jalapeno in a sealed jar for 48 hours. Strain out jalapeno and seeds. Store in a sealed container until ready to use.

SERRANO CHILI INFUSION– use ½ sliced serrano chili

HABANERO CHILI INFUSION– use 2 slices

The longer you leave in the chili, the hotter the infusion.

BERRY GOOD INFUSED VODKA

1 bottle (750 ml) vodka
2 pints strawberries
1 pint raspberries
1 lime, sliced

In a large pitcher add vodka, strawberries, raspberries and sliced lime. Cover and infuse in the refrigerator for 72 hours. Stir occasionally. Strain out fruit and keep refrigerated until ready to use.

No, I can't go jogging with you.

It will make my lunch spill.

BERRY GOOD INFUSED VODKA

BLOODY MARY VODKA INFUSION

1 bottle (750 ml) vodka
½ lemon
½ lime
½ teaspoon white peppercorn
1 jalapeno
6 green olives
6 Kalamata olives

Clean and slice the lemon and lime. Slice the jalapeno in half. In in large sealable container combine ingredients and infuse for 48 hours. Keep refrigerated until ready to use.

Infusion-Collusion

(See "Infused Spirits" for these recipes)

A negative person sees the glass half empty, a positive person sees the glass half full. A realistic person adds two shots of vodka, some ice and says, "Cheers."

BERRY GOOD LEMONADE

2 ounces berry good infused vodka

4 ounces lemonade

strawberries

raspberries

1 lime

mint

Combine ingredients in a glass. Garnish with a strawberry, raspberries, 1 slime slice and mint.

STARBURST-TINI

1 ½ ounces strawberry Starburst infused vodka

1 ½ ounces sweet and sour mix

unwrapped strawberry Starburst

Combine ingredients in a shaker half-filled with ice and shake the crap out of it until the drink is well blended and chilled. Strain into a Martini glass or over ice. Garnish with a Starburst on a pick.

PROJECT PINEAPPLE 101

2 ounces pineapple infused vodka

1 ounce coconut vodka

3 ounces lemonade

¼ ounce cream of coconut

pineapple wedge for garnish

mint for garnish

Combine ingredients in a shaker half-filled with ice and shake the crap out of it until the drink is well blended. Strain into a glass half-filled with ice. Add mint and garnish with a pineapple wedge.

PUCKER UP AND KISS ME-TINI

1 ounce green apple infused vodka

½ ounce orange liqueur

1 ounce sweet and sour mix

apple slice for garnish

lemon juice (for apple slice)

Combine ingredients in a shaker half-filled with ice and shake the crap out of it until the drink is well blended and chilled. Strain into a Martini glass. Garnish with an apple slice that has been dipped in lemon juice. (This keeps the apple from turning brown.)

PROJECT PINEAPPLE 101

MAMA CALIENTE

1 ½ ounces chili-infused tequila
½ ounce orange liqueur
1 ounce pineapple juice
1 ounce orange juice
1 ounce sweet and sour mix
1 red chili

Combine ingredients in a shaker half-filled with ice and shake the crap out of it until the drink is well blended and chilled. Strain into a Martini glass. Add a red chili to the rim.

BASIL LEMON DROP

1 ½ ounces basil infused vodka
½ ounce orange liqueur
1 ½ ounces sweet and sour mix
1 teaspoon lemon juice
lemon slice and piece of fresh basil for garnish

Combine ingredients in a shaker half-filled with ice and shake the crap out of it until the drink is well blended and chilled. Strain into a Martini glass. Garnish with a slice of lemon and a piece of fresh basil.

ROCK MY BOAT GIRLIE-TINI

1 ounce basil infused vodka
1 ounce Absolut Pear Vodka
½ ounce Nellie and Joe's Key Lime Juice
½ ounce simple syrup
lime slice for garnish

Combine ingredients in a shaker half-filled with ice and shake the crap out of it until the drink is well blended and chilled. Strain into a glass half-filled with ice and garnish with a slice of lime.

APPLE JOLLY RANCHER

1 ½ ounces Apple Jolly Rancher infused vodka
1 ½ ounces sweet and sour mix
1 apple flavored Jolly Rancher for garnish

Combine ingredients in a shaker half-filled with ice and shake the crap out of it until the drink is well blended and chilled. Serve as a martini, a shot, or over ice. Garnish with a Jolly Rancher if serving as a martini.

MAMA CALIENTE

CALIENTE GIRLIE-TINI

1 ounce jalapeno infused vodka
½ ounce blue curacao
1 ounce pineapple juice
1 ounce orange juice
jalapeno for garnish

Combine ingredients in a shaker half-filled with ice and shake the crap out of it until the drink is well blended and chilled. Strain into a Martini glass and float a slice of jalapeno on top.

The Friday drink fairy is here and I keep telling her it's too early. She says, "Go ahead and have a drink... I dare you." Well friends, you know how I love a dare.

Liquors and Mixers

Yoga class??? I thought you said, pour a glass.

LIMONCELLO

10 lemons
1 (750 ml) bottle vodka
3 ½ cups water
2 ½ cups sugar

Remove the peel from the lemons in long strips using a vegetable peeler. (Reserve the lemons for later.) Use a sharp knife to remove the white pith from the lemon peels and discard the pith. Place the lemon peels in a two quart pitcher. Pour vodka over the peels and cover with plastic wrap. Steep the lemon peels in the vodka at room temperature for four days.

On the fourth day prepare a simple syrup. Combine the water and sugar in a large saucepan over medium heat and stir until it completely dissolves, about five minutes.

When it has completely cooled, pour the sugar syrup into the vodka mixture. Cover and let it stand overnight at room temperature. Strain the limoncello through a mesh strainer. Discard the peels. Transfer the limoncello to bottles and seal. Refrigerate or freeze until ready to use. (Everclear Grain Alcohol makes a stronger limoncello.)

MOONSHINE #anappleadaymakesmeplay

1 ½ bottles Everclear Grain Alcohol (or vodka)
1 gallon apple juice
1 gallon apple cider
1 cup sugar
1 cup brown sugar
4 cinnamon sticks

Bring apple juice, apple cider, sugars and cinnamon sticks to a boil. Let it cool. Remove cinnamon sticks and add Everclear. Pour into jars. Makes 6 quarts.

Friends bring happiness into your life.
Best friends bring alcohol.

LIMONCELLO

Someone sent me an e-mail about using VODKA for cleaning around the house. It worked! The more I drank the cleaner the house looked.

COFFEE LIQUEUR

3 cups rum
4 cups purified drinking water
2 ½ cups sugar
3 tablespoons instant coffee
1 tablespoon vanilla extract

Boil water, coffee and sugar. Reduce heat and simmer for two hours, stirring frequently. This helps to caramelize the sugar and enhance the flavor. Remove from the heat and let it cool. Add vanilla and rum and stir. Bottle and cap tightly. Dark colored bottles are preferred. If you use clear bottles keep out of direct light.

AMARETTO

2 cups vodka
1 cup water
1 cup white sugar
½ cup brown sugar
2 tablespoons almond extract
2 teaspoons vanilla extract

Combine water and sugars in a saucepan and heat until the mixture is boiling and the sugar is dissolved. Remove from the heat and let it cool. Add vodka, almond extract, and vanilla. Stir. Store in a sealed bottle.

IRISH CREAM

2 cups Irish whiskey
1 ¼ cups half-and-half
1 can sweetened condensed milk (14 ounces)
2 tablespoons instant coffee
2 ½ tablespoons chocolate syrup
1 teaspoon almond extract
1 teaspoon vanilla extract

Combine ingredients in a blender and blend on high for approximately thirty seconds. Pour into sealable bottles or jars. Keep refrigerated. Shake well before serving.

(It keeps well in the refrigerator for several months.)

CRANBERRY MIXER

1 cup sugar
1 cup water
2 cups cranberry juice
zest from 1 orange

Combine water and sugar in a sauce pan and cook over medium heat. Stir until the sugar is dissolved. Add cranberry juice and the zest from one orange. Stir, let it cool then strain out the zest using a fine mesh strainer. Refrigerate in a sealed jar or container until ready to use. Perfect for cocktails.

SIMPLE SYRUP

1 cup sugar
1 cup water

Bring water and sugar to a boil, stirring frequently. Reduce to a simmer and stir occasionally until the mixture becomes syrupy. Let it cool. Refrigerate in a covered container for up to two weeks.

Once the sugar dissolves add:

1 cup sliced strawberries to make strawberry simple syrup.

1 cup raspberries to make raspberry simple syrup.

1 cup blueberries to make blueberry simple syrup.

Cook for several additional minutes, remove from heat and let it cool before putting it in a covered container. Refrigerate until ready to use.

SWEET AND SOUR MIX

1 cup sugar
1 cup water
1 cup freshly squeezed lemon or lime juice

Bring water and sugar to a boil, stirring frequently until sugar is dissolved. Remove from heat and let it cool. Add one cup of freshly squeezed lemon or lime juice. Refrigerate in a sealed jar until ready to use. It will last several weeks.

Bloody Mary and her Entourage

Of course I'm feeling better... I'm on my second Bloody Mary!

BLOODY RICH MARY

2 ounces vodka
5 ounces tomato, vegetable or V8 Juice
1 teaspoon Worchestershire Sauce
1 ounce lemon juice
1 teaspoon Tabasco Hot Sauce
¼ teaspoon Dijon Mustard
¼ teaspoon prepared horseradish
¼ teaspoon celery seed
¼ teaspoon minced garlic
¼ teaspoon pepper
pinch of celery salt
lemon slice for rimming and garnish
Lawry's Seasoning Salt for rimming

Add ingredients to a glass half-filled with ice and stir. Garnish with celery stick and any of your favorite garnishes.

TWISTED BLOODY MARY MIX

64 ounce bottle of tomato, vegetable, or V8 Juice
½ cup freshly squeezed lemon or lime juice
2 tablespoons prepared horseradish
1 tablespoon Dijon Mustard
4 tablespoons Worchestershire Sauce
2 tablespoons Tabasco Hot Sauce
2 teaspoons celery seeds
1 teaspoon sea salt
2 teaspoons fresh ground black pepper
2 teaspoons minced garlic

Combine ingredients in a large pitcher and stir.

Add 2 ounces of vodka to a tall glass half-filled with ice. Fill the remaining glass with the twisted Bloody Mary mix and your favorite garnishes.

DIRTY SALT (for glass rimming) Combine coarse sea salt, celery salt, seasoning salt, cayenne pepper, and ground pepper in a plastic bag. Shake well then pour onto a shallow plate large enough for a glass rim.

MOODY MARY

2 ounces jalapeno infused vodka (see Infused Spirits)
5 ounces twisted Bloody Mary mix
lemon wedge for garnish and glass rimming
dirty salt for rimming
celery stick for garnish
garnishes

Moisten the rim of a glass with the lemon wedge, then dip it into the dirty salt.

Add ingredients to a glass half-filled with ice and stir. Garnish with the lemon wedge, celery stick and any of your favorite garnishes.

BLONDE MARY

3 ounces jalapeno infused tequila (see Infused Spirits)
4 ounces twisted Bloody Mary mix
4 ounces Corona Beer
lime wedge for garnish and glass rimming
celery stick for garnish
dirty salt for rimming

Moisten the rim of a glass with a lime wedge, then dip it into the dirty salt.

Combine ingredients in a glass half-filled with ice and stir. Garnish with a celery stick and lime wedge.

FRISKY MARY

2 ounces Triple Crown Whiskey
5 ounces twisted Bloody Mary mix
celery stick
garnishes

Combine ingredients in a glass half-filled with ice and stir. Add a celery stick and your favorite garnishes.

You say tomato, I say Bloody Mary!

SINFUL MARY

2 ounces peppercorn infused vodka (see Infused Spirits)
5 ounces twisted Bloody Mary mix
dirty salt for rimming
lemon wedge for rimming
celery stick

Moisten the rim of a glass with a lemon wedge, then dip it into the dirty salt.

Combine ingredients in a glass half-filled with ice and stir. Garnish with a celery stick and your favorite garnishes.

HARRY CARRY MARY

3 ounces Bloody Mary vodka (see Infused Spirits)
2 cups twisted Bloody Mary mix
¼ teaspoon Sriracha Sauce
garnishes

Combine ingredients in a glass half-filled with ice and stir. Garnish with a celery stick and your favorite garnishes.

BLOODY MARY VODKA, BLOODY RICH MARY,
TWISTED BLOODY MARY MIX, DIRTY SALT

9

#

Oops...I bought Champagne instead of milk...again?

PINK PRINCESS

chilled Champagne
½ ounce orange liqueur
¼ cup chilled cranberry juice

Combine triple sec and cranberry juice in a shaker half-filled with ice and shake the crap out of it until the drink is well blended and chilled. Strain one ounce into your Champagne glass and top with Champagne.

THE DAZZLER

1 ounce chilled Hpnotiq Liqueur
chilled Champagne

Pour chilled Hpnotiq and Champagne into a glass and stir.

LEMONY FIZZ

#bestbrunchchampagnecocktailohyeah
chilled Champagne
3 ounces citron vodka
1 pint lemon sorbet

Combine vodka and lemon sorbet in a blender and blend until smooth. Fill a Champagne or wine glass with one-third of the mixture and top with Champagne. Stir. Serves 6.

RAZZAMATAZZ

1 ounce chilled citron vodka
chilled Champagne
½ ounce blue curacao
½ ounce orange juice

Combine vodka and orange juice in a shaker half-filled with ice and shake the crap out of it until the drink is well blended and chilled. Pour into a Champagne glass, add Champagne and top with blue curacao. Gently stir.

BELLISSIMO

1 ounce chilled limoncello
chilled Prosecco
1 ounce sweet and sour mix
raspberries

Combine six raspberries, limoncello, and sweet and sour mix in a blender and blend until smooth. Pour into a Champagne glass and top with Prosecco. Stir. Garnish with raspberries.

PINK PRINCESS AND THE DAZZLER

PARADISE FIZZ

chilled Champagne
2 ounces coconut rum
½ ounce cream of coconut

Combine coconut rum and cream of coconut in a shaker half-filled with ice and shake the crap out of it until the drink is well blended and chilled. Strain into two Champagne glasses and top with Champagne. Stir.

MMMMMMMMIMOSA

1 bottle chilled Champagne
2 cups chilled orange juice
1 cup chilled pineapple juice
grenadine syrup

Combine orange juice, pineapple juice and Champagne in a large pitcher. Stir. Serve immediately in Champagne glasses. Add a splash of grenadine.

SOUTHERN BELLA BELLINI

2 ounces 360 Georgia Peach Flavored Vodka
1 ounce peach schnapps
1 ounce peach nectar
4 ounces chilled Prosecco
1 ripe peach, peeled and cubed
1 cup ice

Combine ingredients in a blender and blend until smooth. Serve in Champagne glasses. Garnish with a peach slice. Serves 2.

PEACHES AND CRÈME BELLINI

1 ½ ounces Pinnacle Whipped Cream Vodka
1 ounce peach schnapps
3 ounces chilled Prosecco
1 very ripe peach, peeled and cubed
1 teaspoon lemon juice

Combine ingredients in a blender and blend until smooth. Serve in Champagne a glass. Garnish with a slice of peach. To make a frozen peach Bellini, freeze the peach first.

You Silly Girl...there's no such thing as too much Champagne.

If the cashier asks, "How's your day going?" I reply, "I'm buying three bottles of Champagne. It's clearly going to get better."

PEACHES AND CRÈME BELLINI

PINK FIZZY

1 ounce rum
chilled Champagne
splash triple sec
1 ½ ounces ruby red grapefruit juice

Combine the ruby red grapefruit juice, rum, and triple sec in a shaker half-filled with ice and shake the crap out of it until the drink is well blended and chilled. Strain into a Champagne glass and top with Champagne.

CRANBERRY FIZZ

chilled Champagne
splash of orange liqueur
½ tablespoon whole cranberry sauce
1 tablespoon cranberry juice

Add cranberry sauce, orange liqueur and cranberry juice in each glass. Top with Champagne and stir.

MARdi GRAS

HERACAME

3 ounces light rum
½ ounce orange liqueur
4 ounces frozen Guava Passion Orange Juice concentrate
½ ounce lime juice
½ ounce grenadine syrup
orange slice for garnish
Maraschino cherry for garnish

Prepare Guava Passion Orange Juice following directions on container. Combine ingredients in a shaker half-filled with ice and shake the "merde" out of it until the drink is well blended and chilled. Strain into a hurricane glass half-filled with ice. Garnish with a cherry and orange slice.

Then...

HIMACAME

2 ounces dark rum
2 ounces light rum
½ ounce orange liqueur
2 ounces orange juice
2 ounces pineapple juice
½ ounce lime juice
¼ ounce grenadine syrup
lime wedge for garnish
Maraschino cherry for garnish

Combine ingredients in a shaker half-filled with ice and shake the "merde" out of it until the drink is well blended and chilled. Strain into a hurricane glass half-filled with ice. Garnish with a cherry and a lime wedge

Do not serve these drinks back to back. They must be served front to front. (wink wink)

MASKED LADY

1 ounce vodka
1 ounce gin
½ ounce orange liqueur
½ ounce lime juice
1 ounce guava juice
1 ounce orange juice
2 ounces pineapple juice
soda water
mint garnish

Combine ingredients in a goblet filled with ice and stir. Top with soda water. Garnish with mint.

BLUE BAYOU

2 ounces white rum
½ ounce blue curacao
½ ounce coconut cream

Combine ingredients in a shaker half-filled with ice and shake the "merde" out of it until the drink is well blended and chilled. Strain into a Martini glass.

FRENCH QUARTER FIZZ

2 ounces dark rum
4 ounces ginger ale
grenadine syrup
Maraschino cherry for garnish

Combine rum and ginger ale in a glass half-filled with ice and stir. Add a splash of grenadine. Garnish with a cherry.

Laissez les bons temps rouler!
Let the good times roll!

CAJUN GIRLIE-TINI

1 ½ ounces jalapeno infused vodka (see Infused Spirits)
1 ounce dry vermouth
sliced jalapeno pepper for garnish

Combine vodka and vermouth in a shaker half-filled with ice and shake the "merde" out of it until the drink is well blended and chilled. Strain into a Martini glass. Garnish with a jalapeno slice.

Give me lemonade to change the things I can change and girlie-tinis to accept the things I can't.

HIMACAME

HERACAME

CARPE DIEM

2 cups dark rum
2 cups orange juice
2 cups pineapple juice
½ cup sweet and sour mix
grenadine syrup
Maraschino cherry garnish

Combine ingredients in a pitcher and stir. Serve in a glass half-filled with ice. Add a splash of grenadine. Garnish with a cherry.

MARDI GRAS KISS

1½ ounces rum
½ ounce amaretto
½ ounce simple syrup
2 ounces pineapple juice
lemon slice for garnish

Combine ingredients in a shaker half-filled with ice and shake the "merde" out of it until the drink is well blended and chilled. Strain into a glass half-filled with ice. Garnish with a lemon slice.

Besties

Girlfriends forever...
it's me and you
against whatever!

LEFT TO RIGHT: BESTIES FOREVER: JUANITA SPENCER, SUE DETTORRE, JULIE PORTO, KIM CARBONATI, EILEEN BIANCHI, PAT BIRCKHEAD AND VIRGINIA HALVERSON

BESTIE

½ ounce vodka
½ ounce tequila
½ ounce rum
½ ounce gin
½ ounce triple sec
1 ounce sweet and sour mix
2 ounces cranberry juice
2 ounces orange juice
lime wedge for garnish
Maraschino cherry for garnish
besties

Combine ingredients in a shaker half-filled with ice and shake the crap out of it until the drink is well blended and chilled. Strain into a glass half-filled with ice. Garnish with a cherry and lime wedge. Toast to friendship with your bestie!

YA YAS

2 ounces light rum
1 ounce dark rum
1 ounce orange liqueur
1 ounce orange juice
1 ounce pineapple juice
½ ounce sweet and sour mix
½ ounce cream of coconut
grenadine syrup
Maraschino cherry

Combine ingredients in a shaker half-filled with ice and shake the crap out of it until the drink is well blended and chilled. Strain into a pretty glass half-filled with ice. Add a splash of grenadine. Garnish with a cherry.

14

I'm sick and tired of my friends who can't handle their alcohol. The other night they dropped me three times while carrying me home.

CARO AMICO

(dear friend)

1 ounce Stoli Citron Vodka
1 ounce limoncello
½ ounce orange liqueur
1 ounce lemonade
red wine

Combine the vodka, limoncello, orange liqueur and lemonade in a shaker half-filled with ice and shake the crap out of it until the drink is well blended and chilled. Strain into a Martini glass. Pour the red wine slowly over the back of a spoon onto the drink. It will float on top of the drink the entire time.

SOUL SISTER-TINI

1 ½ ounces 360 Georgia Peach Flavored Vodka
¼ ounce amaretto
1 ounce cranberry juice
1 ounce orange juice
1 fresh peach for garnish

Combine ingredients in a shaker half-filled with ice and shake the crap out of it until the drink is well blended and chilled. Strain into a Martini glass. Garnish with a peach slice.

SASSY FRASSY

1 ½ ounces citron vodka
½ ounce blue curacao
2 ounces pineapple juice
½ ounce sweet and sour mix

Combine ingredients in a shaker half-filled with ice and shake the crap out of it until the drink is well blended and chilled. Strain into a Martini glass.

MON AMI

2 ounces vodka
2 ounces pineapple juice
1 ounce raspberry liqueur
1 lemon for garnish

Combine ingredients in a shaker half-filled with ice and shake the crap out of it until the drink is well blended and chilled. Strain into a Martini glass. Garnish with a lemon twist.

PARTNERS IN CRIME

2 ounces Hussong's Platinum Tequila
6 raspberries (plus 1 for garnish)
2 thin slices jalapeno
½ ounce agave syrup
2 ounces ruby red grapefruit juice
½ ounce lime juice
1 cup ice

Combine ingredients in a blender using only one slice of jalapeno and blend until the ice is completely crushed. Pour into a glass then garnish with a raspberry and a slice of jalapeno.

CLIQUE-TINI

2 ounces coconut vodka
1 ounce Montego Bay Coconut Rum
1 cup sliced strawberries (plus 1 for garnish)
3 ounces pineapple juice
¼ ounce cream of coconut
½ cup crushed ice

Combine ingredients in a blender and blend until smooth. Pour in a glass and garnish with a strawberry.

BIRTHDAY GIRLIE-TINI

1 ½ ounces Pinnacle Cake Vodka
chilled champagne
2 ounces cranberry juice cocktail
whipped cream
sprinkles
birthday candles
birthday girl and her besties

Combine vodka and cranberry juice in a shaker half-filled with ice and shake the crap out of it until the drink is well blended and chilled. Strain into a Martini glass. Add a splash of champagne and stir. Top with whipped cream, sprinkles and candles for the birthday girl. Make a wish and let the celebration commence.

bes-tie n. one of several very near and dear friends

Yappy Hour

It looks like you have a lot on your mind.
Let's drink about it.

POMEGRANATE GIRLIE-TINI

1 ½ ounces Stoli Citron Vodka
½ ounce Patron Citronge Orange Liqueur
2 ounces pomegranate juice
juice from a lime wedge
pomegranate seeds for garnish

Combine ingredients in a shaker half-filled with ice and shake the crap out of it until the drink is well blended and chilled. Strain into a Martini glass. Garnish with a few pomegranate seeds.

LIQUID COURAGE

2 ounces 360 Vodka
½ ounce blue curacao
1 ounce pineapple juice
1 ounce orange juice
½ ounce sweet and sour mix
pineapple wedge garnish

Combine vodka, pineapple and orange juice in a shaker half-filled with ice and shake the crap out of it until the drink is well blended and chilled. Strain into a Martini glass. Slowly pour in the blue curacao down the side of the glass. Garnish with a pineapple wedge.

HYPNO-YOLO

1 ounce Hpnotiq Liqueur
1 ounce 360 Vodka
1 ounce lemonade
1 ounce pineapple juice
splash of lemon-lime soda
lemon slice

Combine ingredients in a shaker half-filled with ice and shake the crap out of it until the drink is well blended and chilled. Strain into a glass half-filled with ice and garnish with a lemon slice.

KEY LIME TIME-TINI

2 ounces rum
2 ounces limeade
1 ounce sweet and sour mix
¼ ounce Nellie & Joe's Key West Lime Juice
graham crackers, crushed for rimming
coconut cream for rimming
whipped cream
1 lime for garnish

Rim a Martini glass with the coconut cream, then the crushed graham crackers.

Combine ingredients in a shaker half-filled with ice and shake the crap out of it until the drink is well blended and chilled. Strain into the Martini glass. Garnish with whipped cream and a lime slice.

CELEBRATION-TINI

2 ounces Pinnacle Cake Vodka
½ ounce orange liqueur
¼ cup sliced strawberries
1 cup ice
whipped cream
cake sprinkles

Combine ingredients in a blender and blend until smooth. Pour into a pretty glass. Top with whipped cream and sprinkles.

Everyone needs
a hobby.
Mine is yappy hour!

Womanhood...powered by love, fueled by determination, sustained by girlie-tinis!!!

POMEGRANATE GIRLIE-TINI

PLAN B
(when PLAN A fails)

1 ounce rum
1 ounce Montego Bay Coconut Rum
1 ounce frozen limeade concentrate
½ ounce coconut cream
1 cup of crushed ice
lime slice for garnish

Combine ingredients in a blender and blend well. Pour into a glass. Garnish with a lime slice.

IN KAHOOTS GIRLIE-TINI

2 ounces 360 Georgia Peach Flavored Vodka
1 ounce Montego Bay Coconut Rum
½ ounce peach schnapps
1 ripe peach
1 ounce sprite
½ cup ice

Peel and dice one half of a peach and combine with vodka, rum, sprite and ice in a blender and blend until smooth. Pour into a Martini glass. Garnish with a peach slice.

PEARED-UP GIRLIE-TINI

1 ounce Absolut Pear Vodka
1 ounce Absolut Vodka
1 ounce pear nectar
1 lime
1 pear for garnish

Combine ingredients in a shaker half-filled with ice and shake the crap out of it until the drink is well blended and chilled. Strain into a Martini glass. Add juice from half of a lime. Garnish with a pear slice.

17

Group Therapy

HELL YA!

4 cups Hussong's Platinum Tequila
1 cup orange liqueur
2 cups orange juice
2 cups pineapple juice
1 cup sweet and sour mix
1 orange for garnish

Combine ingredients in a pitcher and stir. Serve over ice. Garnish with an orange slice. Serves 8.

MY THERAPIST

1 cup 360 Vodka
1 cup rum
1 cup gin
1 cup Hussong's Platinum Tequila
1 cup orange juice
1 cup pineapple juice
1 cup cranberry juice
2 cups sweet and sour mix
Maraschino cherries for garnish

Combine ingredients in a large pitcher and stir. Pour into a glass half-filled with ice. Garnish with a cherry. Serves 10.

HELL YA!

TINKY TINGLERS

1 (750 ml) bottle white rum
½ cup McCormick Triple Sec
12 ounces frozen limeade concentrate
3 cups water
1 lime for garnish
mint for garnish

Combine ingredients in a large pitcher and stir until well blended. Serve over ice. Garnish with a lime wedge and mint sprig. Serves 6.

GROUP THERAPY

3 cups rum
1 cup Montego Bay Coconut Rum
2 cups cranberry juice
2 cups pineapple juice

Combine ingredients in a pitcher and stir. Serve as a girlie-tini or over ice. Serves 6.

Cocktails are cheaper than therapy and you don't need an appointment!

ATTITUDE ADJUSTMENT
3 cups Triple Crown Whiskey
1 cup McCormick Triple Sec
1 cup orange juice
1 cup pineapple juice
1 cup sweet and sour mix
1 cup ginger ale soda
grenadine syrup
1 orange for garnish

Combine ingredients, except for the grenadine, in a pitcher and stir. Serve over ice. Add a splash of grenadine. Garnish with an orange slice. Serves 6.

COVERT MISSION
2 cups Hussong's Reposado Tequila
½ cup Gran Gala Liqueur
2 cups tonic water
1 cup sweet and sour mix
½ cup lime juice
2 limes for garnish
coarse sea salt for rimming

Combine ingredients in a pitcher and stir. Serve over ice in a margarita glass rimmed with salt. Garnish with a lime wedge. Serves 4.

OPERATION RECOVERY
3 cups Hussong's Reposado Tequila
¾ cup McCormick Triple Sec
4 cups ruby red grapefruit juice
5 ounces frozen limeade concentrate

Mix ingredients in a large pitcher and stir until well blended. Serve over ice. Serves 8.

HAPPY JUICE
2 cups light rum
½ cup Montego Bay Coconut Rum
¼ cup blue curacao
3 cups pineapple juice

Combine ingredients in a pitcher and stir until well blended. Serve as a girlie-tini or over ice. Serves 6.

Sometimes getting out of the house seems like a covert mission.

It's Been A Hellava Day

Remedies provided

50 SHADES OF BLUE

2 ounces Hpnotiq
1 ounce blue curacao
½ ounce sweet and sour mix
2 ounces tonic water
Maraschino cherry for garnish
blackberry

Combine ingredients in shaker half-filled with ice and shake the hell out of it until the drink is well blended and chilled. Slide a blackberry onto the pick and attach the cherry onto the bottom of the pick. Add ice to the glass and sip away.

50 SHADES OF BLUE

HELLAVA DAY

1 ½ ounces bourbon
¾ ounce sweet and sour mix
1 ¼ ounces pineapple juice
¼ ounce coconut cream
grenadine syrup
Maraschino cherry for garnish
an upbeat song

Play an upbeat song. Combine ingredients in a shaker half-filled with ice and shake the hell out of it until the drink is well blended and chilled. Strain into a glass half-filled with ice. Add a splash of grenadine. Garnish with a cherry. Ahh...your day can only get better.

MIDDLE FINGER

2 ounces gin
¼ ounce orange liqueur
2 ounces ruby red grapefruit juice
sprig of rosemary for garnish

Combine ingredients in a shaker half-filled with ice and shake the hell out of it until the drink is well blended and chilled. Strain into a Martini glass. Garnish with a sprig of rosemary. Dare to do the salute with a drink in hand.

#phecalphreak #thebosswhocrapsonyourday

2 ounces dark rum
2 ounces orange juice
2 ounces lemon-lime soda
½ ounce tablespoon sweet and sour mix
grenadine syrup
orange slice for garnish
Maraschino cherry for garnish

Combine ingredients, except for lemon-lime soda, in a shaker half-filled with ice and shake the hell and crap out of it until the drink is well blended and chilled. Strain into a glass half-filled with ice. Add lemon-lime soda and a dash of grenadine. Garnish with an orange slice and cherry. Oh Crap!

I've learned to use meditation and relaxation to handle stress....
Just kidding...I'm on my second girlie-tini.

PMS
(Pissy Mood Syndrome)
2 ounces Pinnacle Whipped Vodka
2 ounces coconut rum
¼ ounce blue curacao
2 ounces pineapple juice
2 ounces orange juice
½ ounce coconut cream

Combine ingredients in a shaker half-filled with ice and shake the hell out of it until the drink is well blended and chilled. Strain into a Martini glass or serve over with ice. Get out of my way until I've calmed down!

IT'S A LOONG STORY
½ cup citron vodka
2 ounces pineapple juice
1 ounce sweet and sour mix
1 ounce half and half
1 ounce lemon juice
1 ounce cream of coconut
1 cup ice
lime wedge for garnish

Combine ingredients in a blender and blend until smooth. Pour into a glass and garnish with a lime wedge. Serves 2. Now it's times to tell your story.

BAMBOOZLED
1 ounce light rum
1 ounce coconut rum
1 ounce coffee liqueur
2 scoops vanilla ice cream
chocolate jimmies for glass rimming
chocolate syrup

Rim a pretty glass with chocolate syrup, then dip into the chocolate jimmies.

Combine ingredients in a blender and blend until smooth. Serve in the pretty glass.

50 SHADES OF RED

WTF?
1 ounce rum
1 ounce vodka
½ ounce orange liqueur
1 ounce orange juice
1 ounce sweet and sour mix
½ ounce cranberry juice
orange slice for garnish

Combine ingredients in a shaker half-filled with ice and shake the hell out of it until the drink is well blended and chilled. Strain into a glass half-filled with ice. Garnish with an orange slice.

50 SHADES OF RED
(for when it's just not your day)
2 ounces citron vodka
½ ounce orange liqueur
1 ounce sweet and sour mix
3 ounces pomegranate juice
light corn syrup
granulated sugar
pomegranate seeds for garnish
Dip your Martini glass in the syrup, then the sugar.

Combine ingredients in a shaker half-filled with ice and shake the hell out of it until the drink is well blended and chilled. Strain into a Martini glass. Add pomegranate seeds.

ATTITUDE ADJUSTMENT

IF LIFE WERE EASY WE WOULDN'T NEED GIRLIE-TINIS.

TIME OUT
2 ounces 360 Mandarin Orange Flavored Vodka
1 ounce 360 vodka
1 ounce orange juice
1 ounce pineapple juice
¼ ounce sweet and sour mix
orange slice for garnish

Combine ingredients in a blender half-filled with ice and shake the crap out of it until the drink is well blended and chilled. Strain into a Martini glass.

#begenerous #numberonefunnygirl

NAUGHTY GIRL
1 ½ ounces Pinnacle Blood Orange Flavored Vodka
½ ounce blue curacao
2 ounces white cranberry juice
lemon slice for garnish

Combine ingredients in a shaker half-filled with ice and shake the crap out of it until the drink is well blended and chilled. Strain into a Martini glass. Garnish with a lemon slice.

DECOMPRESSION
1 ½ ounces 360 Vodka
1 ounce 360 Sorrento Lemon Flavored Vodka
2 ounces cranberry juice
½ ounce sweet and sour mix
strawberry for garnish

Combine ingredients in a shaker half-filled with ice and shake the crap out of it until the drink is well blended and chilled. Strain into a Martini glass. Garnish with a strawberry.

MOMMY WATER #mommytakes2olivesinherwater
2 ounces Stoli Vodka
¼ ounce Gallo Extra Dry Vermouth
2 martini olives

Combine the ingredients in a shaker half-filled with ice and shake the crap out of it until the drink is well blended and chilled. Strain into a Martini glass. Garnish with two olives on a cocktail pick.

HELL YA
2 ounces Hussong's Reposado Tequila
½ ounce McCormick Triple Sec
2 ounces orange juice
1 ounce pineapple juice
1 ounce sweet and sour mix
orange wedge for garnish

Combine the ingredients in a shaker half-filled with ice and shake the crap out of it until the drink is well blended and chilled. Strain into a Martini glass. Garnish with an orange wedge.

TIME OUT, NAUGHTY GIRL, DECOMPRESSION AND MOMMY WATER

#berrysmashed

2 ounces Triple Crown Whiskey
chilled Champagne
1 cup lemonade
¼ cup blueberries plus some for garnish
lemon slice for garnish
1 garnish pick

Muddle ¼ cup blueberries in a glass. Add whiskey, lemonade and a ½ glass of ice. Top with Champagne and stir. Garnish with a row of blueberries on a pick and a lemon slice. Substitute blackberries or strawberries for blueberries.

#begenerous #numberonefunnygirl

1 ½ ounces coconut vodka
2 ounces pineapple juice
½ ounce coconut cream
1 cup ice
pineapple wedge
Maraschino cherry

Slice the cherry in half. Carve just enough pineapple out of the back side so that the cherry can be inserted.

Combine ingredients in a blender and blend until smooth. Pour into a glass. Garnish with the pineapple wedge.

Whew...I had a moment where I thought I needed a man...but I was able to open the whiskey bottle myself.

IT'S ALL ABOUT ME

1 ounce vodka
1 ounce rum
½ ounce peach schnapps
½ ounce orange liqueur
2 ounces orange juice
2 ounces pineapple juice
1 ounce lemon-lime soda
orange slice for garnish

Combine ingredients in a glass half-filled with ice and stir. Garnish with an orange slice.

23

Taking my best shot!

YOWZA
3 ounces vodka
1 ½ ounces blue curacao
1 ounce sweet and sour mix
1 lemon

Combine ingredients in a shaker half-filled with ice and shake the crap out of it until the drink is well blended and chilled. Strain into 4 shot glasses. Serve with a lemon wedge.

PARTY GIRL SHOOTER
1 ½ ounces vodka
½ ounce blue curacao
2 ounces cranberry juice

Combine ingredients in a shaker half-filled with ice and shake the crap out of it until the drink is well blended and chilled. Strain into two shot glasses.

TRANSFORMATION
½ ounce bourbon
½ coffee liqueur
½ ounce Irish cream

Combine ingredients in a shaker half-filled with ice and shake the crap out of it until the drink is well blended and chilled. Strain into a shot glass.

WOMAN'S HONOR
{taste like a thin mint}
1 ounce 360 Double Chocolate Vodka
½ ounce coffee liqueur
½ ounce Irish cream
½ ounce peppermint schnapps

Combine ingredients in a shaker half-filled with ice and shake the crap out of it until the drink is well blended and chilled. Strain into two shot glasses.

HOT DAMN!

Why I drink?
If you met my family you'd understand!

SLUTTY PROFESSOR

1 ounce vodka

1 ounce Frangelico Liqueur

1 ounce Irish cream

Combine ingredients in a shaker half-filled with ice and shake the crap out of it until the drink is well blended and chilled. Strain into two shot glasses.

RED HEADED FLOOZIE

1 ounce vodka

½ ounce peach schnapps

1 ounce cranberry juice

Add ingredients to a shaker half-filled with ice and shake the crap out of it until the drink is well blended and chilled. Strain into a shot glass.

BIRTHDAY CAKE

1 ounce Pinnacle Cake Vodka

1 ounce Irish cream

whipped cream

sprinkles

candle

Combine vodka and Irish cream in a shaker half-filled with ice and shake the crap out of it until the drink is well blended and chilled. Strain in a shot glass, add whipped cream, sprinkles and a candle.

YOWZA

KAPOWWWW

2 ounces Triple Crown Whiskey

½ ounce orange liqueur

1 ounce orange juice

1 ounce cranberry juice

Combine ingredients in a shaker half-filled with ice and shake the crap out of it until the drink is well blended and chilled. Strain into 4 shot glasses.

HOT DAMN!

2 ounces Fireball Whiskey

½ ounce Triple Crown Whiskey

½ ounce sweet and sour mix

1 ounce cranberry juice

Marashino cherries with stems

rimming sugar

light corn syrup

Rim each shot glass with corn syrup, then rimming sugar.

Combine ingredients in a shaker half-filled with ice and shake the crap out of it until the drink is well blended and chilled. Strain into 4 shot glasses. Put a small slit in the bottom of each cherry and attach it onto the rim of the glass.

25

THE YOUNG & THE RECKLESS

I can't really talk the talk or walk the walk, but if you need someone to drink the drink, I'm your girl!

left to right: #karaaaazygirlietini, #girlshavingfun, #selfietini.
Back row: #partygirls, #ms.snarky

#karaaaazygirlietini

1 ½ ounces tequila
½ ounce Patron Citronge Orange Liqueur
2 ounces cranberry juice
½ ounce fresh lime juice

Combine ingredients in a shaker half-filled with ice and shake the crap out of it until the drink is well blended and chilled. Strain into a Martini glass.

#girlshavingfun

2 ounces bourbon
raspberry liqueur
2 ounces cranberry juice
1 ounce sweet and sour mix

Combine bourbon, cranberry juice and sweet and sour mix in a shaker and shake the crap out of it until the drink is well blended and chilled. Strain into a glass. Add a splash of raspberry liqueur.

#selfietini

2 ounces rum
½ ounce orange liqueur
3 ounces ruby red grapefruit juice

Combine ingredients in a shaker half-filled with ice and shake the crap out of it until the drink is well blended and chilled. Strain into a Martini glass.

#ms.snarky

2 ounces bourbon
1 ounce Sour Apple Schnapps
3 ounces cranberry juice

Combine ingredients in a shaker half-filled with ice and shake the crap out of it until the drink is well blended and chilled. Strain into a glass.

#partygirls

1 ounce vodka
1 ounce limoncello
2 ounces cranberry juice

Combine ingredients in a shaker half-filled with ice and shake the crap out of it until the drink is well blended and chilled. Strain into two shot glasses or serve as a martini.

And then my girlie-tini said, "Put that on Facebook, it's hilarious." But my girlie-tini was wrong...so very wrong!

#winkydinkytini

2 ounces citron vodka

1 teaspoon raspberry liqueur

3 ounces lemonade

raspberries for garnish (optional)

lemon twist for garnish

Combine ingredients in a shaker half-filled with ice and shake the crap out of it until the drink is well blended and chilled. Strain into in a Martini glass. Garnish with raspberries or a lemon twist.

#craycraygirlietini

1 ½ ounces rum

½ ounce Patron Citronge Orange Liqueur

3 ounces pomegranate juice

Combine ingredients in a shaker half-filled with ice and shake the crap out of it until the drink is well blended and chilled. Strain into a Martini glass.

#twofacedgirlietini

1 ounce citrus vodka

1 ounce limoncello

½ ounce Patron Citronge

1 ounce lemonade

red wine

Combine the vodka, limoncello, orange liqueur and lemonade in a shaker half-filled with ice and shake the crap out of it until the drink is well blended and chilled. Strain into a Martini glass. Pour the red wine slowly over the back of a spoon and it will float on top of the drink the entire time.

#twittermetini

2 ounces vodka

2 ounces orange juice

2 ounces cranberry juice

orange slice for garnish

Maraschino cherry for garnish

Combine ingredients in a shaker half-filled with ice and shake the crap out of it until the drink is well blended and chilled. Strain into a Martini glass. Garnish with a cherry or slice of orange.

#twistedtini

3 ounces citron vodka

2 ounces sweet and sour mix

2 ounces tonic water

1 lime for garnish

2 Maraschino cherries

Combine ingredients in a shaker half-filled with ice and shake the crap out of it until the drink is well blended and chilled. Strain into two glasses half-filled with ice. Squeeze a lime wedge into each drink. Garnish with a lime slice and cherry. Serves 2.

#twistedtini

Dear Alcohol,

We had a deal where you would make me funnier, smarter, and a better dancer.

I saw the video...we need to talk.

The Break Up

It is best to have loved and lost
than to live with a PSYCHO for the rest of your life.

PSYCHO

1 ounce bourbon
1 ounce vodka
½ ounce orange liqueur
2 ounces orange juice
1 ounce sweet and sour mix
orange slice for garnish
Maraschino cherry
picture of the dirty bastard

Combine ingredients in a glass and stir.
Garnish with an orange slice and cherry.

Take a sip of your drink then spit it all over the
psycho's picture.

PSYCHO

OXYMORON

2 ounces dark rum
2 ounces Southern Comfort
2 ounces pineapple juice
2 ounces cranberry juice
grenadine syrup
Maraschino cherry for garnish
BFF

Combine ingredients, except for grenadine, in a
cocktail shaker half-filled with ice and shake the crap
out of it until the drink is well blended and chilled.
Strain into a tall glass half-filled with ice. Add a
splash of grenadine. Garnish with a cherry.

Tell your BFF why the ex is a SOB, then clink and
drink.

DIRTY BASTARD

1 ounce light rum
1 ounce dark rum
½ ounce triple sec
1 ounce orange juice
1 ounce cranberry juice
1 ounce pineapple juice
1 ounce lemon-lime soda
lemon wedge for garnish
paper and markers
besties

Combine ingredients, except for soda, in a shaker
half-filled with ice and shake the crap out of it until
the drink is well blended and chilled. Strain into a
glass half-filled with ice and top with lemon-lime soda.
Garnish with a lemon wedge.

Use the paper and markers to draw a picture of what
this dirty bastard looks like. Make it a group project
and see who comes up with the best picture.

MR. EVIL

1 ounce vodka
1 ounce gin
½ ounce orange liqueur
4 ounces orange juice
grenadine syrup
lime wedge for garnish

Combine vodka, gin and orange juice in a shaker half-filled with ice and shake the crap out of it until the drink is well blended and chilled. Strain into a glass half-filled with ice. Add a splash of grenadine and garnish with a lime wedge.

JEKYLL AND HYDE

1 ounce vodka
1 ounce gin
1 ounce rum
½ ounce orange liqueur
3 ounces strawberry lemonade
2 ounces lemon lime soda
strawberry for garnish
mint sprig for garnish

Combine ingredients, except for soda, in a shaker half-filled with ice and shake the crap out of it until the drink is well blended and chilled. Strain into a glass half-filled with ice. Add lemon lime soda and stir. Garnish with a strawberry and mint sprig.

WRECKING BALL

1 ounce rum
1 ounce bourbon
2 ounces sweet and sour mix
1 ounce pineapple juice
½ lime
mint sprig for garnish

Combine rum, bourbon, sweet and sour mix, and pineapple juice in a shaker half-filled with ice. Add the zest of one lime, then the juice of ½ of a lime. Shake the crap out of it until the drink is well blended and chilled. Strain your drink into a glass half-filled with ice. Garnish with a mint sprig.

DOUCHE BAG

2 ounces gin
½ ounce orange liqueur
1 ounce orange juice
1 ounce pineapple juice
½ ounce Rose's Sweetened Lemon Juice
lime wedge for garnish
pen and paper

Combine ingredients in a shaker half-filled with ice and shake the crap out of it until the drink is well blended and chilled. Strain into a glass half-filled with ice. Garnish with a lime wedge.

Make a list of all the things you will do without this douche bag in your life.

PAINKILLER

2 ounces gold rum
2 ounces pineapple juice
1 ounce orange juice
1 ounce sweet and sour mix
½ ounce cream of coconut

Combine ingredients in a shaker half-filled with ice and shake the shake the crap out of it until the drink is well blended and chilled. Strain into a glass half-filled with ice. Add a sprinkle of nutmeg.

NEVER get jealous when you see your ex with someone else, because our parents taught us to give our USED TOYS to the LESS FORTUNATE!

SUMMERTIME HEATWAVE

Today's forecast: hot...with occasional cocktails.

EASY PEASY LEMON SQUEEZY

3 cups citron vodka

2 cups lemonade

2 cups sweet and sour mix

4 lemons

mint sprig

Combine ingredients in a pitcher and stir. Serve in a glass half-filled with ice. Cut a lemon into wedges and squeeze one into each drink. Garnish with a lemon slice and mint sprig. Serves 6.

KEY LIME DREAM

3 ounces light rum

2 ounces coconut cream

2 ounces pineapple juice

1 ½ ounces Nellie & Joe's Key West Lime Juice

1 ½ cups ice

pineapple wedge for garnish

Combine ingredients in a blender and blend until smooth. Pour into a glass and garnish with a pineapple wedge.

BUZZ PATROL

2 ounces light rum

1 ounce coconut rum

2 ounces orange juice

1 ounce sweet and sour mix

lemon slice for garnish

Combine ingredients in a shaker half-filled with ice and shake the crap out of it until the drink is well blended and chilled. Strain into a glass half-filled with ice. Garnish with a lemon slice.

SPIKED GRANITA

2 cups vodka

1 cup orange liqueur

4 cups watermelon

sweet and sour mix

Puree first 3 ingredients in a blender. Pour into a shallow dish and freeze for several hours. When ready to serve spoon into a glass and add 1 ounce of sweet and sour mix. Garnish with a small wedge of watermelon. Serve with a spoon and straw. Serves 8.

EASY PEASY LEMON SQUEEZY, KEY LIME DREAM, BUZZ PATROL

SLUSHY HUSSY

1 ½ cups vodka

12 ounces frozen pink lemonade concentrate

3 ounces frozen orange juice concentrate

4 cups cold water

2 lemons

In a large bowl combine lemonade, orange juice, vodka, water and the zest from one lemon. Stir thoroughly, then pour mixture into a freezer-safe container. Freeze overnight. Stir once halfway through the freezing process. To serve, stir, then spoon into glasses. Garnish with a lemon slice. Serves 6.

RISKY WHISKEY SLUSH

6 cups Triple Crown Whiskey

2 cups brewed tea (4 teabags)

6 ounces frozen orange juice concentrate

12 ounces frozen lemonade concentrate

2 ¼ cups hot water

½ cup sugar

6 cups water

1 orange

First, prepare 2 cups of brewed tea using 4 teabags. Let it cool. Boil 2 ¼ cups of hot water. Add frozen orange juice, frozen lemonade, brewed tea and stir. Pour into a large freezer safe glass pitcher or plastic container.

Add whiskey, sugar and 6 cups water. Stir with a plastic, glass or wooden spoon. (Metal changes the taste). Freeze for 48 hours. Spoon into a glass and garnish with an orange slice. Serves 12.

DELIZIOSO

3 ounces chilled Prosecco

1 ounce chilled limoncello

3 raspberries for garnish

mint sprig for garnish

Combine Prosecco and limencello in a wine glass. Stir. Garnish with raspberries and mint.

I'm an outdoorsy kind of girl...in that I like my drinks by the pool.

SUMMER COOLER

½ cup citron vodka

4 12 ounce bottles Corona beer

1 cup frozen pink lemonade concentrate

1 cup strawberries

Muddle 1 cup of strawberries. Mix Coronas, pink lemonade and vodka in a pitcher. Add strawberries and stir. Serve immediately.

SUN-KISSED ALL OVER

3 cups tequila

¾ cup orange liqueur

2 cups pineapple juice

2 cups orange juice

grenadine syrup

Combine ingredients in a large pitcher and stir. Serve in a glass half-filled with ice. Add a splash of grenadine. Serves 6.

JIGGLE JUICE

3 cups coconut vodka

1 cup pineapple juice

1 cup orange juice

1 cup ruby red grapefruit juice

½ cup sweet and sour mix

¼ cup cream of coconut

1 orange for garnish

Combine ingredients in a pitcher and stir until well blended. Serve over ice. Garnish with a slice of orange. Serves 4.

Girlie-ritas Señoritas

These girlie-ritas pair well with nachos and difficult relatives.

SINFUL-RITA

1 ½ cups Hussong's Platinum Tequila
½ cup McCormick Triple Sec
¼ cup sweet and sour mix
2 cups cranberry juice
orange slice for garnish

Combine ingredients in a shaker half-filled with ice and shake the crap out of it until the drink is well blended and chilled. Strain into a glass half-filled with ice. Garnish with an orange slice. Serves 4.

TWISTED-RITA

2 ½ cups Hussong's Platinum Tequila
½ cup McCormick Triple Sec
3 cups prepared limeade
lime slice for garnish

Combine ingredients in a large pitcher. Serve over ice. Garnish with a lime slice. Serves 4.

FIESTY-RITA

2 ounces Tarantula Azul Tequila
1 ounce McCormick Triple Sec
1 ounce sweet and sour mix
1 orange
1 lemon
1 lime

Cut an orange in half and squeeze the juice of half of the orange into a shaker. Cut the lemon and lime into wedges and squeeze the juice of 2 lime and 2 lemon wedges into the shaker. Fill the shaker half way with ice, then add tequila, triple sec and sweet and sour mix. Shake the crap out it until the drink is well blended and chilled. Strain into a glass half-filled witch ice. Garnish with an orange slice.

32

FLIRTY GIRLIE-RITA

3 ounces Hussong's Platinum Tequila
¼ ounce McCormick Triple Sec
½ cup sweet and sour mix
1 ounce Nellie and Joe's Key West Lime Juice
½ ounce coconut cream
2 cups ice
lime wedge for garnish

Combine ingredients blender and blend until smooth. Garnish with a lime wedge.

STRAWBERRY GIRLIE-RITA

1 cup Hussong's Reposado Tequila
¼ cup McCormick Triple Sec
6 ounces frozen limeade concentrate
2 cups fresh strawberries or 3 cups frozen strawberries (thawed)
2 cups crushed ice
lime slice for garnish

Combine ingredients in a blender and blend until smooth. Pour into margarita glasses. Garnish with a lime wedge. Serves 4.

SINFUL-RITA, TWISTED-RITA, FIESTY-RITA

GUAVA JALAPENO GIRLIE-RITA

Life handed me limes instead of lemons,

so I made a pitcher of Girlie-Ritas.

SORBET-RITA

2 ounces Hussong's Platinum Tequila
½ ounce Gran Gala Liqueur
1 cup lemon sorbet
lime wedge

Combine ingredients in a blender and blend until smooth. Serve in a margarita glass. Garnish with a lime wedge.

COVERT MISSION GIRLIE-RITA

2 ounces Hussong's Reposado Tequila
½ ounce McCormick Triple Sec
½ ounce sweet and sour mix
2 ounces tonic water
½ ounce lime juice
coarse sea salt to rim glass
lime wedge

Combine ingredients in a shaker half-filled with ice and shake the crap out of it until the drink is well blended and chilled. Strain into a salt rimmed margarita glass half-filled with ice. Garnish with a lime wedge.

GUAVA JALAPENO GIRLIE-RITA

1 cup Hussong's Platinum Tequila
½ cup McCormick Triple Sec
2 cups guava juice
¼ cup lime juice
1 jalapeno, sliced
coarse sea salt to rim glass
1 lime to rim glasses

Combine ingredients in a pitcher and let it sit for 10-15 minutes. Strain out jalapenos. Serve in salt rimmed margarita glasses half-filled with ice. Garnish with a slice of jalapeno. 2 servings.

GIRLIE-RITA SWEET AND SOUR MIX

1 cup freshly squeezed lime juice, 10-12 limes
1 cup sugar
1 cup water

Bring water and sugar to a boil, stirring frequently until sugar is dissolved. Remove from the heat and let it cool. Add one cup of freshly squeezed lime juice. Refrigerate in a sealed jar for up to two weeks.

33

Sassy Girls Sangrias

OH SO EASY SANGRIA

1 bottle red wine
4 cups lemonade
12 ounces of lemon-lime soda (1 can)
1 lemon, sliced
1 lime, sliced
1 orange, sliced
1 cup blueberries
1 cup strawberries
cherries for garnish
mint for garnish

Mix ingredients in a pitcher and stir. Add fruit. Cover and refrigerate until ready to serve. Garnish with a cherry and mint sprig. Serves 6.

BERRY-LICIOUS SANGRIA

1 bottle red wine
12 ounces frozen raspberry lemonade concentrate
3 cups ginger ale
1 cup blueberries
1 cup blackberries
1 cup raspberries
1 cup strawberries, sliced

Combine ingredients in a large pitcher and stir. Add berries. Cover and refrigerate 4-6 hours before serving. (Frozen berries can be substituted for fresh). Serves 6.

SILLY GIRL SANGRIA

1 bottle burgundy wine
½ cup orange liqueur
2 cups orange juice
2 cups pineapple juice
¼ cup lemon juice
1 lemon, sliced
1 lime, sliced
1 orange, sliced

Combine ingredients in a large pitcher and stir. Add sliced fruit. Cover and refrigerate 4-6 hours before serving. Serves 8.

SASSY SANGRIA

1 bottle red wine
½ cup peach brandy
½ cup orange liqueur
¼ cup lime juice
1 cup sparkling water
1 orange, sliced
1 lime, sliced
1 lemon, sliced
1 peach, sliced or cubed

Combine ingredients in a pitcher and stir. Add fruit. Cover and refrigerate 4-6 hours before serving. Serves 6.

PARTY HARDY SANGRIA

1 bottle red wine
1 cup gin
1 12 ounce can pineapple chunks with juice
2 cups ginger ale
1 cup orange juice
6 ounces frozen lemonade concentrate
½ cup simple syrup
1 orange, sliced
1 lemon, sliced
1 lime, sliced
1 cup strawberries, sliced

Combine ingredients in a large pitcher and stir. Add strawberries and fruit. Cover and refrigerate for 8 hours before serving. Serves 8.

Some people don't respect age until it's bottled.

BEACH BABY SANGRIA

(a tropical style sangria)
1 bottle white wine
1 cup coconut rum
1 12 ounce can pineapple chunks with juice
2 cups pineapple juice
2 cups orange juice
½ cup cream of coconut
1 orange, sliced
1 lemon, sliced
pineapple wedges for garnish

Combine ingredients in a pitcher and stir. Add fruit. Cover and refrigerate for several hours before serving. Garnish with a pineapple wedge. Serves 8.

MA-MA-MIA-SANGRIA

1 bottle white wine
1 cup tequila
½ cup agave nectar syrup
¼ cup lime juice
2 cups lemon-lime soda
1 lemon
1 lime
1 orange
12 fresh mint leaves

Muddle mint leaves in the agave nectar syrup. Combine ingredients in a large pitcher and stir. Add cut fruit. Cover and refrigerate 4-6 hours before serving. Serves 6.

SANGRIA SANGRIA SANGRIA

1 bottle white wine
½ cup orange liqueur
1 cup peach schnapps
1 cup orange juice
12 ounces lemon lime soda
1 tablespoon lime juice
¼ cup club soda
2 peaches, cubed
1 lime, sliced

Combine ingredients in a pitcher and stir. Add fruit. Cover and refrigerate 4-6 hours before serving. Serves 6.

JUST PEACHY SANGRIA

1 bottle white wine
1 cup peach schnapps
1 cup pineapple juice
½ pineapple, cut into wedges
2 peaches, cubed
1 cup strawberries, sliced
1 lemon, cubed
mint

Muddle the mint in 1 tablespoon of pineapple juice. Combine ingredients in a pitcher and stir. Add fruit. Cover and refrigerate 4-6 hours until ready to use. Serves 6.

OH SO EASY SANGRIA

I have discovered the fountain of youth and it looks and tastes just like Sangria!

Feeling Punchy

Of course size matters...no one wants a small glass of punch!

ANY TIME PUNCH
2 (750 ml) bottles vodka
2 cups orange liqueur
64 ounce bottle cranberry juice
4 cups orange juice
1 liter bottle ginger ale
½ cup lemon juice
1 lemon, sliced
1 lime, sliced
1 orange, sliced

Combine ingredients in a punch bowl or drink dispenser and stir. Add fruit. (If it's a winter punch add cranberries).

BUNKO BREW
1 (750 ml) bottle rum
2 cups spiced rum
2 cups orange liqueur
2 cups orange juice
2 cups cranberry juice
2 cups pomegranate juice
2 cups sweet and sour mix
1 orange
1 lemon
1 lime

Combine ingredients in a punch bowl or drink dispenser and stir. Add sliced fruit.

GIRLS GONE WILD
1 (750 ml) bottle rum
2 cups dark rum
1 cup coconut rum
3 cups ginger ale
2 cups pineapple juice
2 cups orange juice
½ cup frozen lemonade concentrate
pineapple chunks
1 orange, sliced
1 lime, sliced

Combine ingredients in a punch bowl or drink dispenser and stir. Add fruit. Serve over ice.

LIL' BIT O' FUN
4 cups rum
3 cups coconut rum
3 cups pineapple juice
2 cups lemonade
2 cups sweet and sour mix
1 lemon, sliced
½ pineapple, chunked

Combine ingredients in a punch bowl or drink dispenser and stir. Add fruit.

RUMALICIOUS PUNCH
4 cups white rum
2 cups orange juice
3 cups pineapple juice
¾ cup limeade concentrate
grenadine syrup
2 oranges for garnish

Combine ingredients in a punch bowl or drink dispenser and stir. Pour into individual glasses. Add a splash of grenadine. Garnish with an orange slice.

RUMALICIOUS PUNCH

RISKY WHISKEY SOUR PUNCH

4 cups Triple Crown Whiskey
5 cups orange juice
1 ½ cups sweet and sour mix
club soda
1 orange
Maraschino cherries for garnish
grenadine syrup

Combine whiskey, orange juice, and sweet and sour mix in a drink dispenser or punch bowl and stir. Serve in a glass half-filled with ice and top with a splash of club soda. Add a splash of grenadine. Garnish with a cherry and orange wedge.

THEMACAME PUNCH #agoodtimeforall

1 (750 ml) bottle rum
1 (750 ml) bottle dark rum
2 cups orange liqueur
3 cups orange juice
2 cups pineapple juice
2 cups lemonade
½ cup lemon juice
grenadine syrup
2 oranges for garnish
Maraschino cherries for garnish

Combine ingredients in a drink dispenser or punch bowl and stir. Serve over ice. Add a splash of grenadine and garnish with an orange slice and cherry.

This punch is a great conversation starter.

"Trust me, you can dance!"

said my glass of punch.

Dessert Me!

GUILTY PLEASURE #chocolatestrawberrydream

1 ounce Tequila Rose Strawberry
2 ounces 360 Double Chocolate Flavored Vodka
1 ounce tequila
4 strawberries
1 cup vanilla ice cream
whipped cream
mint sprig for garnish
chocolate syrup

Squirt some chocolate syrup into the inside of a glass. Refrigerate until ready to use.

Combine Tequila Rose Strawberry, chocolate vodka, tequila, 3 sliced strawberries and ice cream in a blender and blend until smooth. Pour into a prepared glass. Top with whipped cream and chocolate syrup. Garnish with a strawberry and mint sprig.

STRAWBERRY SHORTCAKE #toogoodtopassup

2 ½ ounces Tequila Rose Strawberry
1 ½ ounces 360 Glazed Donut Flavored Vodka
½ cup strawberries, plus one for garnish
whipped cream

Combine ingredients in a blender and blend until smooth. Pour into a Martini glass and top with whipped cream. Garnish with a strawberry.

LEMON PIE- GIRLIE-TINI

1 ½ ounces 360 Sorrento Lemon Flavored Vodka
1 ounce 360 Vodka
½ ounce sweet and sour mix
whipped cream
1 lemon

Combine liquid ingredients in a shaker half-filled with ice and shake the crap out of it until the drink is well blended and chilled. Strain into a Martini glass. Top with whipped cream and add lemon zest.

DESSERTEDLY YUMMY

1 ounce Glazed Donut Flavored Vodka
1 ounce 360 Double Chocolate Vodka
1 ounce Irish Cream
½ ounce amaretto
½ ounce Montego Bay Coconut Rum
1 ounce half and half
chocolate syrup for rimming
grated coconut for rimming

Rim a Martini glass with chocolate syrup, then dip into the coconut. Chill until ready to use.

Combine ingredients in a shaker half-filled with ice and shake the crap out of it until the drink is well blended and chilled. Strain into the Martini glass.

MUDDY BUDDY

1 ½ ounces 360 Vodka
1 ½ ounces 360 Double Chocolate Vodka
3 ounces coffee liqueur
3 ounces Irish cream
2 cups vanilla ice cream
chocolate syrup for garnish
whipped cream
mint sprig for garnish

In two dessert glasses swirl some chocolate syrup around the inside of the glass. Chill until ready to use.

Combine first five ingredients in a blender and blend until smooth. Pour into the glasses. Top with whipped cream, chocolate syrup and a mint sprig.

SIN-UPON

1 ½ ounces RumChata
1 ½ ounces Fireball Whiskey

Combine ingredients in a shaker half-filled with ice and shake the crap out of it until the drink is well blended and chilled. Strain into a glass half-filled with ice.

I use to think eating dessert was bad for me...so now I drink them!

DIRTY FOOL

1 ounce coffee liqueur
1 ounce Irish cream
1 ounce Frangelico Liqueur
2 ounces half and half
coffee beans for garnish

Combine ingredients in a shaker half-filled with ice and shake the crap out of it until the drink is well blended and chilled. Strain into a Martini glass or serve over ice. Garnish with a few coffee beans.

NAUGHTY BEDTIME STORY

4 ounces Triple Crown Whiskey
2 ounces Hershey's Dark Chocolate Syrup
2 cups vanilla ice cream
1 naughty bed time story

Chill two wine glasses.

Combine ingredients in a blender and blend until smooth. Serve in the frosted wine glasses, then share your naughty bedtime story.

OMG

1 ounce 360 Double Chocolate Vodka
1 ounce Irish Cream
1 ounce coffee liqueur
coffee bean ice cream
cocoa nibs

Roast the cocoa nibs in a small sauce pan on medium heat for 5 minutes. Set aside to cool. (No oil is necessary).

Combine the vodka, Irish cream, and coffee liqueur in a shaker half-filled with ice and shake the crap out if it. Put two scoops of ice cream in a parfait glass. Strain the drink over the ice cream. Top with the roasted cocoa nibs. Serves 4.

NIGHT CAP

1 ½ ounces 360 Double Chocolate Vodka
1 ½ ounces RumChata

Combine ingredients in a shaker half-filled with ice and shake the crap out of it until the drink is well blended and chilled. Strain into a Martini glass.

GUILTY PLEASURE #chocolatestrawberrydream

39

My Chocolate Affair

FEELING KOOKY

CARDINAL SIN

1 ounce crème de cacao
1 ounce Hussong's Platinum Tequila
1 ounce Irish cream
1 ounce half and half

Combine ingredients in a shaker half-filled with ice and shake the crap out of it until the drink is well blended and chilled. Strain into a Martini glass.

Every woman has that "crazy bat-shit" gene inside them. It just takes the right man and mix of alcohol to bring it out!

OPERATION DAMSEL IN DISTRESS

1 ounce 360 Vodka
1 ounce 360 Double Chocolate Vodka
2 ounces coffee liqueur
1 ounce Irish cream
1 ounce half and half (or milk)
chocolate syrup
light corn syrup
cocoa powder
chocolate shavings

Dip the glass into the corn syrup, then the cocoa powder. Swirl some chocolate syrup in the Martini glass.

Combine coffee liqueur, vodkas and half and half in a shaker half-filled with ice and shake the crap out of it until the drink is well blended and chilled. Strain into a Martini glass. Top with chocolate shavings.

CA-RAAZY CORRUPTION

½ ounce rum
½ ounce crème de cacao
½ ounce coffee liqueur
½ ounce cream of coconut
1 ounce half and half
grated coconut for rimming
chocolate syrup for rimming

Rim your Martini glass with chocolate syrup, then dip the rim into the coconut. Chill until ready to use.

Combine ingredients in a shaker half-filled with ice and shake the crap out of it until the drink is well blended and chilled. Strain into a Martini glass.

If I was dating myself I would surprise myself with a chocolate martini everyday at 5:00 ... and I would think it was adorable.

ALMOND TOFFEE MARTINI

1 ounce caramel vodka
1 ounce 360 Double Chocolate Vodka
1 ounce amaretto
1 ounce toffee syrup
chocolate syrup for glass rimming
caramel syrup for inside of glass
crushed almonds for glass rimming

Rim a Martini glass with chocolate syrup, then dip the rim into the crushed almonds. Form a decorative design inside the glass with the caramel and chocolate syrups. Refrigerate to chill.

Combine the vodkas, amaretto, and toffee syrup in a shaker half-filled with ice and shake the crap out of it until the drink is well blended and chilled. Strain into the glass.

TOFFEE SYRUP

½ cup brown sugar
½ cup water
1 teaspoon butter

Combine ingredients in a small sauce pan over medium heat and stir frequently until the sugar dissolves, about five minutes. Set aside to cool.

WHISKEY BUSINESS

1 ounce Triple Crown Whiskey
1 ounce 360 Double Chocolate Vodka
½ ounce white crème de cacao
¼ ounce white crème de menthe
½ ounce half and half (or milk)
mint sprigs for garnish

Combine ingredients in a shaker half-filled with ice and shake the crap out of it until the drink is well blended and chilled. Strain into a glass half-filled with ice. Garnish with a mint sprig.

MOUNDS OF JOY GIRLIE-TINI

1 ounce 360 Double Chocolate Vodka
½ ounce Montego Bay Coconut Rum
1 ounce coffee liqueur
1 ounce Irish cream
1 teaspoon coconut cream
shredded coconut for rimming
chocolate syrup for rimming

Rim your Martini glass with chocolate syrup, then dip the rim into the coconut. Chill until ready to use.

Combine the ingredients in a shaker half-filled with ice and shake the crap out of it until the drink is well blended and chilled. Strain into the Martini glass.

To make it a JOYFUL ALMOND GIRLIE-TINI add ½ ounce of amaretto to the recipe.

FEELING KOOKY

2 ounces 360 Double Chocolate Vodka
1 ounce crème de cacao
1 ounce Irish Cream
2 ounces half and half
2 scoops vanilla ice cream
4 chocolate cookies

Combine the vodka, crème de cacao, half and half, 2 cookies and ice cream in a blender and blend until smooth. Pour into a glass. Garnish with one crumbled cookie and 1 whole cookie.

OPERATION DAMSEL IN DISTRESS

Coffee with
Necessary Variables

ROYAL FRAPPE

ROYAL FRAPPE
2 ounces 360 Double Chocolate Vodka
2 ounces coffee liqueur
¾ cup very strong cold coffee
1 cup low fat milk
2 tablespoons granulated sugar
2 cups ice
3 tablespoons Hershey's Chocolate Syrup
whipped cream
coffee beans for garnish

Combine ingredients in a blender and blend until smooth. Serve in a glass and top with whipped cream and coffee beans.

SWEET INSANITY
1 ounce 360 Double Chocolate Vodka
2 ounces Irish cream
½ ounce Frangelica Liqueur
1 scoop chocolate ice-cream
1 tablespoon chocolate syrup
2 ounces coffee, cooled

Combine ingredients in a blender and blend until smooth. Serve in a glass coffee mug. Garnish with a piece of your favorite chocolate. For Easter: A chocolate bunny. Valentine's Day: a heart shaped chocolate. Christmas: a chocolate Santa.

My life used to be 50% wondering if it's too late to drink coffee and 50% wondering if it's too early to drink alcohol. Solution...combine them. Problem solved!

DOMINATRIX

1 ounce Irish cream
1 ounce RumChata
1 ounce white crème de cacao
1 cup hot coffee
whipped cream
chocolate syrup

Add ingredients to a cup of hot coffee. Top with whipped cream and chocolate syrup.

NECESSARY VARIABLES

1 ounce 360 Double Chocolate Vodka
½ ounce white crème de cacao
½ ounce Irish cream
½ ounce amaretto
½ teaspoon coconut cream
1 cup hot coffee
whipped cream
caramel syrup

Add ingredients to a cup of coffee and stir. Top with whipped cream and caramel syrup.

NUTTY GIRL COFFEE

1 ounce 360 Double Chocolate Vodka
1 ounce coffee liqueur
½ ounce Frangelico Liqueur
1 cup hot coffee
whipped cream
chocolate syrup

Add ingredients to a cup of hot coffee and stir. Top with whipped cream and chocolate syrup.

CHOCOLATE ECLAIR

1 ounce 360 Double Chocolate Vodka
1 ounce crème de cacao
1 ounce Irish cream
½ ounce coffee liqueur
1 cup hot coffee
whipped cream
chocolate syrup

Add ingredients to a cup of hot coffee and stir. Top with whipped cream and chocolate syrup.

DOMINATRIX, NECESSARY VARIABLES, NUTTY GIRL COFFEE

43

WE ARE PUBLISHED BECAUSE OF THESE PEOPLE BELOW!

First, we would like to thank our "Tasteologists", Cathy Bianchi, Pat Birckhead, Sue Dettorre, Virginia Halverson, Julie Porto, and Juanita Spenser for spending most of their Friday nights for over a year dedicated to tasting our concoctions. Without your friendship, honest opinions, sense of humor, and inspiration our vision for CONCOCTOLOGY 101 wouldn't be what it is. Also, we want to thank Leslie Randall, Julie Porto and Pat Birckhead for their editing advice.

To our photographers, John Gray and Erick Bianchi, we thank you for your time, talent and creativity for some of the photographs in our book.

As concoctionists, we used dozens of products. One of our favorite finds was the 360 Double Chocolate Vodka, which we used for our chapters, My Chocolate Affair, Dessert Me, Christmas Spirits, and Coffee with Necessary Variables. When we contacted 360 to ask if we could use their product name in our book, Stephanie Pechar called and wanted to hear more about our book. She loved our concept and sent additional 360 product, along with product from McCormick Distilling. We love your product and especially your Eco-friendly 360 bottles with their flip top lids. We have recycled them for our homemade liqueurs. Thank you Stephanie and McCormick Distilling for your support!

Another huge thank you goes to our dear friends, Shannon and Jason Adams, Jan and Dave Gressman, Patricia and Scott Schrock, Sarah and Chris Stradtner, and Diane and Jim Thompson, for letting us use your homes for photo shoots. We would also like to extend a sincere thank you to John Paolone, Co-Executive at Café Firenze, for letting us do our "Bestie" photograph at this amazing restaurant.

Here's a shout out to the amazing friends in our lives who have helped to shape our personalities and who have made our lives rich beyond measure. We can't thank you enough for the memories we have of you and the good times shared. These lifelong friendships have been the inspiration for dozens of recipes in our book.

To our family, we thank you for your support during this two year process. It was always heartwarming to hear you ask to taste our concoctions and to know we had your love and support!

Lastly, we were so fortunate to find our extremely talented graphic artist, Lauren Alexandra, who took our recipes, photographs and sayings and transformed them into amazing layouts. We are so grateful for your vision, enthusiasm, creativity, hard work and patience. You truly took our vision for this book and made it a reality. Lauren's resume below speaks volumes about her amazing abilities.

Lauren created the national and international print ads that appeared in People, Vanity Fair, Essence, Elle and Connoisseur magazines for Michael Jordan's fragrance line, developed while working with the exclusive men's label, Bijan of Beverly Hills. She served as the Art Director for The California Apparel News & directed fashion shoots for the weekly newspaper and five regional magazines. She held the position of Senior Art Director for Martin Lawrence Galleries and created the first "Don't Bungle The Jungle" campaign for pop icon Madonna. In addition, she has worked as a professor at The Fashion Institute of Design & Merchandising (where she holds a degree in addition to her Bachelor of Arts degree from California State University, Northridge), among many other professional artistic accomplishments including magazine designs featuring Frank Sinatra, George Burns, Princess Diana, Madonna, and The Beatles. Lauren is currently the Design Department Director at Hancock University. Lauren can be contacted at laurenalexandra9@gmail.com.

Notes:

Made in the USA
San Bernardino, CA
08 June 2016